YOUR KNOWLEDGE HAS VALUE

Bibliographic information published by the German National Library:

The German National Library lists this publication in the National Bibliography; detailed bibliographic data are available on the Internet at http://dnb.dnb.de .

Imprint:

Copyright © 2017 GRIN Verlag
Print and binding: Books on Demand GmbH, Norderstedt Germany
ISBN: 9783668972858

This book at GRIN:

https://www.grin.com/document/489358

Danielle Kyle

Federalist and Neofunctionalist Integration Theories in Times of Crisis

A Literature Review

GRIN Verlag

GRIN - Your knowledge has value

Since its foundation in 1998, GRIN has specialized in publishing academic texts by students, college teachers and other academics as e-book and printed book. The website www.grin.com is an ideal platform for presenting term papers, final papers, scientific essays, dissertations and specialist books.

Visit us on the internet:

http://www.grin.com/

http://www.facebook.com/grincom

http://www.twitter.com/grin_com

Federalist and Neofunctionalist Integration Theories in Times of Crisis: A Literature Review

Danielle Kyle

Table of Contents

Abstract

In the past few years, the European Union has seen three major crises; the Schengen crisis, the euro crisis and Brexit. Though all of these events are individual and unique unto themselves, what similarities do they have? What can European integration theories do in order to help us understand their similarities and differences?

In this review, I compare federalist and neo-functionalist literature on crisis outcomes in the EU. I seek to answer the posed questions and see which argument upholds best against Brexit, a crisis which is not yet in the post-crisis phase.

Introduction

As the European Union faces new challenges, integration theorists have had the opportunity to conduct new research. It is an optimal time to present different integration theories as explanations for the cause of EU crises, but also as a proposed way to prevent them. As an intergovernmental organization, the European Union has to work in a way that pleases and accommodates many different countries. Which integration theory can best explain the outcomes of European Union (EU) crises?

As a result of the UK's vote to leave the EU, and prominent candidates in other member states using the possibility of EU withdrawal as a platform, the EU is repeatedly described as being at a crossroads. So, it is essential to understand some of the relevant literature from various integration theories in order to also understand the information the EU can use as it determines its future.

This review aims to compare the strength of argument posed by two pieces of literature, each in favor of a different integration theory. The literature should be able to provide clarity to how these crises came about, as well as plausible explanations for their aftermath. The chosen literature presents federalist and neofunctionalist theories in "a decade of crises" (Schimmelfennig, 2018). While there will be some discussion of the euro crisis and the Schengen crisis, this review will focus on the most recent EU crisis: Brexit.

All of the texts are very recent in order to account for the modern context necessary to understand these events. If the literature of one integration theory literature is better at describing and accounting for the variation in crises, then it should be applicable to literature that does not favor one integration theory over others.

This literature review is formatted as follows: first, presenting relevant historical context as to not deter from the main purpose of comparing the literature in light of modern events, using the literature to define each key concept, reviewing the literature and finally comparing the literature to draw conclusions.

Background

First, it is essential to know how the past may provide parallels to the current debates facing the EU.

Tracing back to the 20th Century, Altiero Spinelli and Friedrich Hayek provided Europe with views on federalism. While neither of them were specifically the cause of early European integration, both did provide food for thought and lay down a framework that would inspire other integration theories - such as Jean Monnet's neo-functionalism (Reho, 2017).

Reho's *The past and future of European federalism: Spinelli vs. Hayek* analyzes and compares the two federalist perspectives, keeping in mind the state of the EU in 2017 while he explains the different viewpoints in their current time. Like many other researchers on the subject, Reho asserts, in a rephrased manner, that the European Union is at a crossroads and how they proceed can make or break it. He describes federalism as "one of the most abused political concepts in European integration," so this article is likely to provide clarification for the possibilities of federalism in the European Union. He proposes that Spinelli's federalism "influenced the past of European integration" and Hayek's "may be able to shape the future" (Reho, 2017).

2

Hayekian federalism only acknowledges what Reho describes as "negative [economic] integration" where economic activities are unregulated. Hayek focused on "continental openness, rather than a central European government" (Reho, 2017). Conversely, Spinelli provided a much more socialist outlook for an integrated Europe. He and Hayek provided two very extreme sides of federalism's possibilities - Spinelli seeking intervention to its full extent and Hayek seeking to keep intervention at a minimum. In reference to the aforementioned misuse of federalism in European integration, Reho essentially says that Spinelli ignores some of the key aspects of a federalist perspective in spite of (Spinelli) trying to defend them (Reho, 2017). It appears that, due to his dismissal of Spinelli's current relevance, Reho has a bias in favor of Hayek's views on federalism which continues to shape the article. He does present both Hayek and Spinelli in equal time, but does little to refute any of Hayek's views, especially given how much Reho counters Spinelli's federalist theories. As far as providing the necessary background to understand how the birth of the EU affects its present arguments, Reho does a fine job in spite of his bias. He does credit neo-functionalism as the founding principle of the European Union, but also explains that Spinelli and Hayek's federalism have a strong influence. Despite all of the differing views on federalism, Reho suggests "as much union as necessary, as little union as possible" as the motto of "authentic federalism" (Reho, 2017).

The UK's position in Europe has always been a bit different, and perhaps the same sentiment can be extended towards the UK's position in the European Union. As Brexit is one of the latest crises facing the EU, involving circumstances the European Union has not yet seen before, it is important to have some background on why the UK would be the only country to choose to leave the European Union thus far. Before exploring the more recent causations *How British was the Brexit Vote?* provides, it is essential to understand earlier viewpoints and how the Brexit decision may have been long coming, via years of built up EU skepticism (and debatably, resentment) (De Burca, 2018).

In order to do so, De Burca stresses Britain's defined, detached politics and culture. It can be understood that Britain's decisive independence from continental Europe is an integral part of its culture, as well (2018). As such, the nature of an intergovernmental organization such as the European Union, even with a motto "United in Diversity," was always going to walk a fine line in regards to providing room for cultural individuality. This applies dually so for the United Kingdom, which anchors much of its culture on its (perceived) distinction from the rest of Europe. In accordance with this, it should be unsurprising that French President Charles de Gaulle was so opposed to the UK having a vote in the EEC, on the basis of the UK wanting to join for economic advantages instead of a true interest in European integration (De Burca, 2018). De Burca seems to agree with this proposal, as she states that "European trajectory has been...ever closer as a union," and highlights that it did begin as a common market project (2018). *How British was the Brexit Vote?* hints that the UK's older, post-war voters, who accounted for more of the "leave" votes than their younger counterparts, did so because they shared the sentiment of a shared economic venture (De Burca, 2018). It seems that Reho's interpretation of Hayek's economic-focused federalism may have been what the UK desired and could have possibly prevented the UK from leaving the EU.

Key Concepts

Federalism

First, I will be using the definition provided by *The past and future of European federalism: Spinelli v. Hayek* in order to shape the rest of the literature review (Reho, 2017). In summary: authentic federalism is defined by Reho with the motto "as much union as necessary, as little union as possible" (2017).

Bergmann and Niemann's 2013 *Theories of European Integration and European Foreign Policy* explains that federalism can mean many things in many different contexts. The authors establish that federalist integration theories provide why states should form a federation, instead of how to go about it (Bergmann, Niemann 2013). Bergmann and Niemann's work provides all integration theories in the same article, where many others choose to focus on one or two alone.

Neo-functionalism

It is asserted that neo-functionalism assumes that integration is a process, which implies that integration happens organically, and over time, many supranational factors shape regional integration, and decisions are motivated primarily by self-interest (Bergmann, Niemann 2013). Neo-functionalism is defined by integration via "spillover" which comes in three forms: functional, political, and cultivated (Bergmann, Niemann 2013). Political spillover involves elites, unable to solve problems domestically, gradually learning to change their expectations, political activities and loyalties to "a new European centre" (Bergmann, Niemann 2013). Functional spillover is when only integration can meet a certain objective (Bergmann, Niemann

2013). And finally, cultivated spillover is when supranational institutions encourage integration in order to increase their own power (Bergmann, Niemann 2013).

Liberal Intergovernmentalism

Intergovernmentalism proposes that European integration is a result of states' interests and bargaining within the EU (Bergmann, Niemann 2013). Where intergovernmentalism says that national interests appear through the state's view of where it stands relative to other states, liberal intergovernmentalism says preferences emerge from the state's politically domestic context (Bergmann, Niemann 2013). Intergovernmentalism defines the source of integration as states' interests and therefore, the states with the most power in bargaining determine that further integration will benefit them (Bergmann, Niemann 2013).

Literature Review

European integration theory in the time of crisis. A Comparison of the euro and Schengen crises. by Frank Schimmelfennig, as implied in the title, compares two recent crises faced by the EU (2018). He makes a strong case for the similarity of the conditions and threats posed by the two crises, in order to show that they are comparable, but wishes to explain why the outcomes were so different. His main argument is that neofunctionalist theories provide the best explanation for the variation in the outcome of the euro crisis and the Schengen crisis.

Schimmelfennig's methodology involves first describing three theories of European integration (intergovernmentalism, post-functionalism, and neo-functionalism), so the reader is familiar with other possible explanations for the variation in the outcome of crises (2018). This

6

was a wise decision, as presenting the other possibilities and their weaknesses shows that Schimmelfennig did consider them before coming to his conclusions. The adaptation of another researcher's* model helps to lessen the likelihood of bias, as Schimmelfennig has not entirely created it on his own and this application is not specifically created in favor of his hypothesis. This is evident in the fact that it was originally a model used as "a liberal-intergovernmentalist explanation of integration [during crises] as the outcome of international interdependence and intergovernmental constellation of preferences and bargaining power," and was not originally used for a neofunctionalist explanation of integration (Schimmelfennig, 2018).

* Leuffen *et al.* 2013

Schimmelfennig goes on to explain liberal intergovernmentalism (LI), which he states does not have a separate model to distinguish between times of crisis and times without (2018). As previously referenced from Bergmann, Nieman 2013, Schimmelfennig refers to national interest, unbalanced interdependence and the strength of institutions in LI's model. Schimmelfennig is sure to counter all main points of LI, which eliminates it as the best explanation for the variation in outcomes between the Schengen crisis and the euro crisis. LI is presented as "Intergovernmentalism: preferences and power," and Schimmelfennig defends this title well, but also provides the reader with why it may not be the best possible answer.

Next, Schimmelfennig presents the neofunctionalist integration theory the rest of this piece of research will rely on (2018). He cites potential holes in the neofunctionalist explanation of integration, though they are all easily believably refuted (Schimmelfennig, 2018). Where liberal intergovernmentalism credits variation in integration outcomes to "the differences in the intergovernmental constellation of preferences and bargaining power and the severity of commitment problems," neo-functionalism "explains the difference in integration outcomes of crises by variation in transnational interdependence and supranational capacity" (Schimmelfennig, 2018). In other words, LI does not appear to have a different model in times of crisis, and its standard model does not withstand the conditions that come about during crises. However, the neofunctionalist explanation of variance in integration outcomes provides a model in times of crises that is easy for the reader to follow and understand. Schimmelfennig's argument that neo-functionalism will best explain the variation in the integration outcomes of the euro crisis and the Schengen crisis remains strong.

In his methodology, Schimmelfennig also provides a comparison of conditions in the euro crisis and the Schengen crisis. The reader is able to understand that both crises involved "shock, failure, conflict and politicization" (2018). Then, Schimmelfennig provides further detail of these conditions. First, 'exogenous shocks': the mortgage crisis in the United States which resulted in a recession and effected European banks, whose government-provided bailouts thereby affected the euro; and the turmoil and conflict plaguing the Middle East as well as questionable conditions in countries that were popular for refugees, which encouraged migration elsewhere - such as the EU member states who were later effected (Schimmelfennig, 2018). He also cites the way these crises revealed the EU's internal defects, which is another 'different yet similar' part of the Schengen crisis and the euro crisis (Schimmelfennig, 2018). While the politicization and conflict caused by the crises is obvious, Schimmelfennig outlining the "shock and failure" is essential to understanding the Schengen crisis and the euro crisis, which makes his research especially relevant to the topic of European integration (2018).

Since the reader is provided with a clear comparison of similarities between the causations of two seemingly different crises, Schimmelfennig has clearly shown why his explanation of the variation in outcomes is necessary. He uses sources from prominent LI scholars, such as Andrew Moravcsik who is also cited by Bergmann, Niemann 2013 as they define LI, which shows that Schimmelfennig sincerely took the LI perspective into account. He also cites Borzel and Risse's *From the Euro to the Schengen crises: European integration theories, politicization, and identity politics*, a prominent postfunctionalist argument on a similar topic. Of course, in drawing his conclusions Schimmelfennig also uses other research in order to support his theory, but the evident consideration of alternate theoretical perspectives distinctively strengthens his argument. Overall, Schimmelfennig goes into great detail, without being redundant, to explain why neo-functionalism best explains the difference in integration outcomes following the euro crisis and the Schengen crisis. *European integration theory in times of crisis: A comparison of the euro and Schengen crises* presents a strongly formulated, well supported argument (Schimmelfennig, 2018). Its strength means that this explanation should also be relevant when applied to other crises facing the EU.

Differentiated integration contingent on objective ability: a federalist critique draws its influence from discussion points in 2017's *White Paper on the Future of Europe* in order to explain "...the aftermath of crises, [in which] there was a shift in the rationale of differentiated integration with objective (in)ability of the states taking a role" (Bardutzky, 2018). His abstract also notes that he will be drawing on the research of Daniel Elazar in order to provide a federal critique of the issues facing the EU in 2017 (Bardutzky, 2018). Similar to Schimmelfennig 2018, it looks at differentiated integration during periods of crisis and post-crisis - but with a federalist gaze as opposed to Schimmelfennig's use of neo-functionalism (Bardutzky, 2018).

Bardutzky's main argument is clearly stated in the opening paragraph of his article - Member States' permission to participate in differentiated integration projects are becoming more reliant on states' ability (2018). As an effect, the divide between the centre and the periphery in the EU "threatens to be reinforced" (Bardutzky, 2018). As previously mentioned, Bardutzky chose to draw primarily on Daniel Elazar's 1987 book *Exploring Federalism*, and accordingly turn a federalist critique on this notion (2018). Using *Exploring Federalism* (Elazar, 1987) in concordance with *White Paper on the Future of Europe* already shows the reader that Bardutzky is using old, respected research in order to make a very modern argument.

He describes the key point of his critique to be Elazar's non-centralization idea of federalism, relying partially on "the guarantee that the authority to participate in exercising powers will not be taken away by sites of power without their consent" (Bardutzky, 2018). Bardutzky believes that participation in integration projects, when reliant on the objective ability of member states, is not in cooperation with Elazar's belief in partnership that holds federal partners accountable (2018). From this, he poses the notion that there should be "a moral commitment between partners in the project of European integration... that should serve as an argument to maintain partnership within a federal project" (Bardutzky, 2018).

Bardutzky's methodology in forming his argument involves first providing the reader with the context necessary to understand it. Like an overwhelming amount of researchers on similar topics in European integration, he begins with "Europe at a crossroads" (Bardutzky, 2018). At this point, I can assume that any literature regarding European integration following the Schengen crisis, the euro crisis, and the Brexit vote will use this context for the reader. While it may seem redundant, it also means that a wide variety of literature is providing the same (or similar) basic background necessary to understand the argument.

Providing the reader with the Brexit vote as context for his argument shows that Bardutzky has chosen to draw on a very recent event, as well as the euro crisis and Schengen crisis mentioned in Schimmelfennig 2018 (2018). While Schimmelfennig states his argument to be post-crisis, Bardutzky describes his own as "somewhere between post-crisis and [midst] crisis (or, crises)" (2018). He utilizes an initial focus on "shock, failure," as was mentioned in Schimmelfennig 2018; namely, the "shock" of a Member State choosing to leave the EU and the "failure" of the EU implied to be "[a lack of] trust, mutual consideration, solidarity, and division of competences" (Bardutzky, 2018). Bardutzky does not outright state them as failures, although stating that those topics need to be discussed and reconsidered in the EU makes it clear that he considers them the EU's downfalls (2018).

"Politicization," in the time following the Brexit vote, involves Eurosceptic platforms becoming a prominent part of 2017 elections in various EU Member States (Bardutzky, 2018). While 2017 will not have been the first time candidates have proposed a withdrawal from the EU, it is the first time they will have done so following the UK's referendum (Bardutzky, 2018). And finally, "conflict" arises in the need for a change in EU policy, at the realization that other Member States may choose to leave, as well (Bardutzky, 2018). This leads into Bardutzky's discussion of *The White Paper on the Future of Europe* (2017), which he credits as the most formal predictions on the future of the EU, from the most credible sources (2018).

As stated earlier, Bardutzky is utilizing the most recent sources and information available to him. On one hand, this can prove to be very effective in its current relevance, but on the other, it can disregard relevant research on previous crises that could be able to support Bardutzky's argument. It is understandable that he would wish to use *The White Paper on the Future of Europe*, especially considering information in the wake of Brexit is relatively limited. However,

Differentiated integration contingent on objective ability: a federalist critique could have benefitted from acknowledging something in between Elazar's *Exploring Federalism* (1987) and *The White Paper on the Future of Europe* (2017) (Bardutzky, 2018).

With that in mind, Bardutzky remains to make a compelling argument in the case of Member States who have weak bargaining power (whether due to their recent EU membership, size, financial (in)ability, etc) - strengthened by his references back to Elazar's work (2018). Additionally, Bardutzky chooses to reference on the weakness in bargaining power for "unwilling Member States" - in other terms, Member States with a trend towards Euroscepticism (2018). He criticizes research that seeks an "ultimate deterrent for noncompliance," such as expulsion from the EU, claiming that the process for doing so can become exclusive (Bardutzky, 2018).

Overall, Bardutzky's federalist critique includes interesting insights to differentiated integration and an imbalance of Member State bargaining power (and more so in times of crisis, which Schimmelfennig previously used to strengthen his argument in favor of neo-functionalism (2018)). However, it appears to have a strong bias in favor of federalism - and, as mentioned in Bergmann and Niemann 2013, Bardutzky's federalist critique focuses on *why* EU Member States should aim to form a federation, as opposed to how Member States could form one. Where Schimmelfennig credits the variation in crisis outcomes to how neo-functionalism "explains the difference in integration outcomes of crises by variation in transnational interdependence and supranational capacity (2018)," Bardutzky credits it to pitfalls of the nature of mankind and believes moral obligation within federalism is strong enough to change integration outcomes (2018).

At this point, Schimmelfennig (2018) presents a more sound scientific argument for neo-functionalism, as an explanation for differentiation in outcomes, than Bardutzky (2018) does in favor of federalism (via his critique). Schimmelfennig (2018) comes across significantly less biased than Bardutzky (2018), with a variety of recent and relevant information provided to support his argument; Bardutzky (2018) relies more on assumptions. The true test of comparison of strength in argument will come next, when both are put to the test on *How British was the Brexit vote?*

How British was the Brexit Vote?(De Burca, 2018) is a concise, yet informative chapter of the book *Brexit and Beyond* (Martill, Staiger, 2018). In this chapter, De Burca aims to determine how much Britain's choice to leave the EU aligns with its history and citizens' beliefs (2018). As mentioned in the background, De Burca notes Britain's contentious past regarding joining an intergovernmental European organization. Particularly, she cites one of French President Charles De Gaulle's reasons for vetoing the UK's request to join the European Economic Community (EEC) in 1963 and 1967 (De Burca, 2018). She claims that De Gaulle's belief that the UK wished to join the EEC for a trading bloc, as opposed to an integrated political community, may have been what played a hand in the UK's eventual withdrawal from the EU (De Burca, 2018). De Burca continues to agree with De Gaulle's belief, noting that the UK did not join the original six Member States of the European Coal and Steel Community in the 1950s due to its preference for prioritizing multilateral free trade and its Atlantic trade partners (2018). She notes the UK joining the EEC a "pragmatic economic choice," and that the decision "was [argued to be] driven by its desire to avoid economic decline," which is why the UK did not seek to do so until the 1960s (2018). Further, she once again reiterates that the UK was likely uninterested in a political venture with the other Member States, naming it an 'awkward partner' regarding its attitude towards the EU (De Burca, 2018). De Burca notes that the UK is exceptional in many ways, but particularly in reference to its "special treatment in relation to the so-called EU budget debate...adopting a pragmatic, case-by-case approach to the introduction of new areas of EU policy" (2018).

In line with Schimmelfennig 2018, *How British was the Brexit vote?* (De Burca, 2018) makes it easy to identify the "shock, failure, conflict and politicization" of Brexit. First, De Burca is sure to examine the exogenous shocks - a global rise in nationalism, illiberal authoritarianism, and distaste for the potential consequences of globalization and immigration (De Burca, 2018). She also notes the similarities between the Brexit movement and Donald Trump's campaign for U.S. president (nationalist sentiment, worries about economic security, anti-immigration, appeal of authoritarian and illiberalism), which can also fall under the category of an 'exogenous shock' for the EU (including the UK) (De Burca, 2018).

Where Bardutzky was concerned with Member State noncompliance resulting in expulsion from the EU, the UK was already seeking to remove itself (2018). This weakens Bardutzky's federalist argument and critique of Brexit.

De Burca also identifies endogenous deficiencies - notably, the EU's immigration policies alienating UK citizens who feared the consequences of immigration (2018). The UK is, notably, not part of the Schengen zone - so in line with De Burca's analysis, an anti-immigration reflex seems very British (2018). As De Burca notes the UK's exceptionalism in its case-by-case analysis and voting in EU policy, she highlights an intergovernmental distributional conflict (Schimmelfennig, 2018); in fact, the same one Bardutzky 2018 highlights - the UK's lack of bargaining power as part of the periphery (2018). And finally, in a mere eight pages De Burca also describes the politicization of the Brexit decision - namely a split between younger and older voters in the UK, and a rise in anti-internationalist populism (2018).

When held to De Burca's claim that 52% of the UK population oppose supranationalism/federalism which they believe the EU to represent (2018), Bardutzky's argument that federalism's moral obligation to partnership should be enough to encourage European integration falls apart (2018). In contrast, Schimmelfennig's argument that neo-functionalism "explains the difference in integration outcomes of crises by variation in transnational interdependence" (such as the UK's desire for less interdependence, potentially motivating its citizens to want to ultimately leave the EU) "and supranational capacity" (2018) (like the EU's ability to allow for the UK's "exceptionalism") stands strong (De Burca, 2018).

Conclusions

Applying theories of integration throughout the course of a crisis can help explain why crises of similar conditions can have variations in outcomes. As the European Union prepares for the UK to officially withdraw, being the first Member State to do so, identifying patterns in crises can help the EU learn from the past, as well as navigate the future.

There are many different theories of integration to compare, but the contrast in research between neofunctionalist and federalist theories of integration made them compelling options. This review highlights the similarities between the euro crisis, Schengen crisis, and Brexit. While there are many comparisons of the former, the latter is relatively new and usually kept to a category of its own.

If the integration concepts of literature on a specific theory can also be applied, relevantly and convincingly, to other literature, it will highlight the strength of the argument. Conversely, if a piece of literature's argument falls apart when applied to a different concept, it is likely a weak argument.

Frank Schimmelfennig *European integration theory in the time of crisis. A Comparison of the euro and Schengen crises* (2018) proposes that neo-functionalism can best explain the variation in outcomes of the euro crisis and the Schengen crisis. He tests his argument in favor of neo-functionalism by presenting the reader with information on why other theories of integration, like post-functionalism and liberal intergovernmentalism, to not explain the variation as well. In doing so, Schimmelfennig proves that his argument stands even when provided with additional information.

Conversely, *Differentiated integration contingent on objective ability: a federalist critique* uses a federalist perspective to explain outcomes of different crises - with an emphasis on Brexit (Bardutzky, 2018). While it is, overall, a critique on the functions of the EU, *Differentiated integration contingent on objective ability: a federalist critique* poses arguments that do not apply as strongly to other articles (Bardutzky, 2018). Bardutzky makes a strong case but his work shows strong bias (in favor of federalism) and does not apply as well to similar arguments.

When Bardutzky (2018) and Schimmelfennig's (2018) arguments were applied to *How British was the Brexit vote?* (De Burca, 2018), the strengths and flaws in both stood out. *How British was the Brexit vote?* did not use a specific integration theory, but rather explained possible causations for the UK's decision to withdraw from the EU (De Burca, 2018). *How British was the Brexit vote?* emphasized the plausibility and thoroughness of Schimmelfennig's (2018) argument, which was where Bardutzky's (2018) argument fell short (De Burca, 2018).

Based on the literature reviewed, Schimmelfennig's neofunctionalist argument in *European integration theory in the time of crisis. A Comparison of the euro and Schengen crises* (2018) has proven to be more applicable and reliable. As such, Schimmelfennig's neofunctionalist explanation of variation in crises outcomes is likely to be more reliable in predicting (and understanding) Brexit outcomes, and the possible paths the EU may take following it, than Bardutzky's (2018) use of the federalist theory of integration.

Bibliography

Bardutzky, Samo. (2018). Differentiated integration contingent on objective ability: a federalist critique. *Perspectives on Federalism*, 10:1.

Börzel, Tanja A. & Risse, Thomas. (2017). From the euro to the Schengen crises: European integration theories, politicization, and identity politics, *Journal of European Public Policy*, 25:1, 83-108, DOI: 10.1080/13501763.2017.1310281

Bergmann, Julian & Niemann, Arne. (2013). Theories of European Integration and their Contribution to the Study of European Foreign Policy. *8th Pan-European Conference on International relations, Warsaw.*

De Búrca, G. (2018). How British was the Brexit vote? In Martill B. & Staiger U. (Eds.), *Brexit and Beyond: Rethinking the Futures of Europe* (pp. 46-52). London: UCL Press. Retrieved from http://www.jstor.org/stable/j.ctt20krxf8.10

Dosenrode, Soren. (2010). Federalism Theory and Neo-functionalism: Elements for an analytical framework. *Perspectives on Federalism,* 2:3.

Reho, Federico Ottavio. (2017). The past and future of European federalism: Spinelli v. Hayek. *European Policy Information Center.*

Schimmelfennig, Frank. (2018). European integration (theory) in times of crisis. A comparison of the euro and Schengen crises, *Journal of European Public Policy*, 25:7, 969-989, DOI: 10.1080/13501763.2017.1421252